MW01105360

ENCOURAGEMENT

— *for* —

TEACHERS

Words of Wisdom and Inspiration

Compiled by
Elizabeth Cody Newenhuyse

HAROLD
SHAW
PUBLISHERS

Wheaton, Illinois

Copyright © 1999 by Harold Shaw Publishers

ISBN 0-87788-618-0

Cover photo © 1999 by John Shaw

05 04 03 02 01 00 99

10 9 8 7 6 5 4 3 2 1

Printed in Colombia

There has never been the slightest doubt in my mind that the God who started this great work in you would keep at it and bring it to a flourishing finish in the very day Christ Jesus appears.

—*Philippians 1:9-10, THE MESSAGE*

CONTENTS

ACKNOWLEDGMENTS

Grateful acknowledgment is made to the publishers of the Scripture versions quoted in this book, using the following abbreviations:

KJV   King James Version
NASB   New American Standard Bible
NIV   New International Version
NKJV   New King James Version
NLT   New Living Translation
NRSV   New Revised Standard Version
RSV   Revised Standard Version
TLB   The Living Bible
THE MESSAGE
Portions from:

The *Holy Bible, 21st Century King James Version* (KJ21®), © 1994, Deuel Enterprises, Inc., Gary, SD. Used by permission.

The New American Standard Bible, © 1960, 1962, 1963, 1968, 1971, 1972, 1973, 1975, 1977 by The Lockman Foundation. Used by permission.

The *Holy Bible, New International Version* ®. NIV ®. © 1973, 1978, 1984 by International Bible Society. Used by permission of Zondervan Publishing House. All rights reserved.

The "NIV" and "New International Version" trademarks are registered in the United States Patent and Trademark Office by International Bible Society. Use of either

INTRODUCTION

Teachers instruct, inspire, impart wisdom, and help shape young lives. They prepare lesson plans, attend meetings, impose discipline, and sometimes dig into their own pockets to pay for needed supplies. In short, much of a teacher's work consists of doing things for others—but teachers, too, need wisdom, inspiration, and refreshment. It is our hope that these words, from Scripture and other sources of wisdom, will provide encouragement amid the busyness and challenge of a teacher's work.

1

FOLLOWING THE
MASTER TEACHER

"I have given you an example to follow: do as I have done to you."
—*John 13:15, TLB*

"Abide in Me, and I in you. As the branch cannot bear fruit of itself, unless it abides in the vine, so neither can you, unless you abide in Me. I am the vine, you are the branches; he who abides in Me, and I in him, he bears much fruit; for apart from Me you can do nothing."
—*John 15:4-5, NASB*

"But seek first his kingdom and his righteousness, and all these things shall be yours as well."
—*Matthew 6:33, RSV*

As a general rule, teachers teach more by what they are than by what they say.
—*Anonymous*

Those of us who are strong and able in the faith need to step in and lend a hand to those who falter, and not just do what is most convenient for us. Strength is in service, not status.
—*Romans 15:1, THE MESSAGE*

And as for you, brothers, never tire of doing what is right.
—*2 Thessalonians 3:13, NIV*

And we pray this in order that you may live a life worthy of the Lord and may please him in every way: bearing fruit in every good work, growing in the knowledge of God, being strengthened with all power according to his glorious might so that you may have great endurance and patience, and joyfully

giving thanks to the Father, who has qualified you to share in the inheritance of the saints in the kingdom of light.
—*Colossians 1:10-12, NIV*

Happy are people of integrity, who follow the law of the Lord. Happy are those who obey his decrees and search for him with all their hearts. They do not compromise with evil, and they walk only in his paths.
—*Psalm 119:1-3, NLT*

The mediocre teacher tells. The good teacher explains. The superior teacher demonstrates. The great teacher inspires.
—*Anonymous*

Don't copy the behavior and customs of this world, but let God transform you into a new person by changing the way you think. Then you will know what God wants you to do, and you will know how good and pleasing and perfect his will really is.
—*Romans 12:2, NLT*

Kids can smell empty words and false feelings a mile away. On the other hand, there is nothing they know better than the scent of sincerity.
—*Cartwright and D'Orso,* For the Children

Trust God from the bottom of your heart. Don't try to figure out everything on your own. Listen for God's voice in every-

thing you do, everywhere you go. He is the one who will keep you on track. Don't assume that you know it all. Run to God! Run from evil!
—*Proverbs 3:5-7, THE MESSAGE*

The first Christians were taught by Jesus, who educated them in the true sense of the word *educare*, "to lead out." The main method of learning was for the community of disciples to follow their mentor or rabbi.
—*Dieter T. Hessel*, Social Ministry

But the fruit of the Spirit is love, joy, peace, patience, kindness, goodness, faithfulness, gentleness, self-control; against such there is no law.
—*Galatians 5:22-23, RSV*

Never pay back evil for evil to anyone. Do things in such a way that everyone can see you are honorable. Do your part to live in peace with everyone, as much as possible.
—*Romans 12:17-18, NLT*

The most important part of the training of the Twelve was one which was perhaps at the time little noticed, though it was producing splendid results—the silent and constant influence of His character on them. It was this which made them the men they became.
—*James Stalker*

Learn as you go along what pleases the Lord.
—*Ephesians 5:10, TLB*

We must prepare and encourage our teachers to be as concerned with their moral manner as they are with their subject-matter methods.

—*Gary D. Fenstermacher*

Some children were brought to Jesus so he could lay his hands on them and pray for them. The disciples told them not to bother him. But Jesus said, "Let the children come to me. Don't stop them! For the Kingdom of Heaven belongs to such as these." And he put his hands on their heads and blessed them before he left.

—*Matthew 19:13-15, NLT*

The greatest use of life is to
spend it for something that will
outlast it.
—*William James*

Think of yourselves the way
Christ Jesus thought of himself.
He had equal status with God
but didn't think so much of himself that he had to claim the ad-
vantages of that status no matter
what. Not at all. When the time
came, he set aside the privileges
of deity and took on the status of
a slave, became *human!* Having
become human, he stayed human. It was an incredibly hum-
bling process. He didn't claim
special privileges. Instead he
lived a selfless, obedient life and
then died a selfless, obedient
death—and the worst kind of

death at that: a crucifixion.

Because of that obedience, God lifted him high and honored him far beyond anyone or anything, ever, so that all created beings in heaven and on earth—even those long ago dead and buried—will bow and worship before this Jesus Christ, and call out in praise that he is the Master of all, to the glorious honor of God the Father.

—*Philippians 2:5-11, THE MESSAGE*

But we have this treasure in earthen vessels, to show that the transcendent power belongs to God and not to us.

—*2 Corinthians 4:7, RSV*

You can't separate yourself as a teacher from yourself as a per-

son. You are all of one piece. And it is good for your pupils that you are. They learn better from a human than they do from a teaching machine.
—*Ruth Beechick,* Teaching Primaries

"There's trouble ahead when you live only for the approval of others, saying what flatters them, doing what indulges them. Popularity contests are not truth contests—look how many scoundrel preachers were approved by your ancestors! Your task is to be true, not popular."
—*Luke 6:26,* THE MESSAGE

Acknowledge and take to heart this day that the Lord is God in heaven above and on the earth below. There is no other. Keep his decrees and commands, which I am giving you today, so that it may go well with you and your children after you and that you may live long in the land the Lord your God gives you for all time.

—*Deuteronomy 4:39-40, NIV*

I have learned to place myself every day before God as a vessel to be filled with the Holy Spirit. He has given me the blessed assurance that he, as the everlasting God, has guaranteed his own work in me.

—*Andrew Murray*

Failure is not sin. Faithlessness is.

—*Henrietta Mears*

In everything you do, put God first, and he will direct you and crown your efforts with success.
—*Proverbs 3:6, TLB*

Since my heart was touched at seventeen, I believe I have never awakened from sleep, in sickness or in health, by day or by night, without my first waking thought being how best I might serve my Lord.
—*Elizabeth Fry*

A good example is the tallest kind of preaching.
—*African proverb*

There are two things to do about the gospel—believe it and behave it.

—*Susannah Wesley*

2

STRENGTH FOR THE DAY'S WORK

Work hard so God can say to you, "Well done." Be a good workman, one who does not need to be ashamed when God examines your work.
—*2 Timothy 2:15, TLB*

Begin school as if you had just heard good news and took pleasure in imparting [it], and keep this up all day.
—*Abbie G. Hall,* Points Picked Up: One Hundred Hints in How to Manage a School

My God, you are always close to me. In obedience to you, I must now apply myself to outward things. Yet, as I do so, I pray that you will give me the grace of your presence. And to this end I ask that you will assist my work, receive its fruits as an offering to you, and all the while direct all my affections to you.
—*Brother Lawrence*

I am only one, but I am one. I can't do everything, but I can do

something. And what I can do,
that I ought to do, and what I
ought to do, by the grace of God,
I shall do.
—*Edward Hale*

May the words of my mouth
and the thoughts of my heart be
pleasing to you, O Lord, my rock
and my redeemer.
—*Psalm 19:14, NLT*

Character grows in the soil of
experience, with the fertiliza-
tion of example, the moisture of
desire, and the sunshine of satisfaction.
—*Anonymous*

But Moses pleaded with the
Lord, "O Lord, I'm just not a

good speaker. I never have been, and I'm not now, even after you have spoken to me. I'm clumsy with words."

"Who makes mouths?" the Lord asked him. "Who makes people so they can speak or not speak, hear or not hear, see or not see? Is it not I, the Lord? Now go, and do as I have told you. I will help you speak well, and I will tell you what to say."
—*Exodus 4:10-12, NLT*

And whatsoever ye do, do it heartily, as to the Lord, and not unto men; Knowing that of the Lord ye shall receive the reward of the inheritance: for ye serve the Lord Christ.
—*Colossians 3:23-24, KJV*

God give us grace to realize that education is not simply *doing* the things we like, *studying* the tasks that appeal to us, or wandering in the world of thought *whither* and *where* we will. . . . It is the *unpleasant* task, the *hard* lesson. . . . that often leads to knowledge and power and good.
—*W. E. B. Du Bois,* Prayers for Dark People

The lure of the distant and the difficult is deceptive. The great opportunity is where you are.
—*John Burroughs*

Give me the ability to see good things in unexpected places and talents in unexpected places. Give me the grace to tell them so.
—*Author unknown*

God is not unjust; he will not forget your work and the love you have shown him as you have helped his people and continue to help them. We want each of you to show this same diligence to the very end, in order to make your hope sure. We do not want you to become lazy, but to imitate those who through faith and patience inherit what has been promised.
—*Hebrews 6:10-12, NIV*

Allow yourself to fail, to forgive failure, and to learn from failures. You won't be right all of the time, you know, but God can use you, even in your weakness, to serve his purposes. Whether you are new . . . or not, your starting point must be the reali-

zation that you are the instrument and God is the strength of your teaching. Ask him, therefore, to renew you daily—even hourly—that you may serve him well. Your commitment to be God's tool will change your focus from performance to praise.
—*Lorna Van Gilst*, Christian Educators Journal

The time of business does not with me differ from the time of prayer. In the noise and clatter of my kitchen, while several persons are at the same time calling different things, I possess God in as great tranquility as if I were on my knees. We should establish ourselves in a sense of God's

presence by continually con-
versing with him.
—*Brother Lawrence*

Like the horizons for breadth
and the ocean for depth, the understanding of a good leader is
broad and deep.
—*Proverbs 25:3, THE MESSAGE*

The world seldom notices who
the teachers are; but civilization
depends on what they do and
what they say.
—*Anonymous*

The school was only 14 by 16
feet. George squeezed in on a
long high bench made of rough
boards. He thought, I can hardly
move. Soon he realized, It is up

to me to do the learning, for the
teacher is too busy keeping order.
—*Neal Stocker*, George Washington
Carver

"Have I not commanded you?
Be strong and courageous! Do
not tremble or be dismayed, for
the Lord your God is with you
wherever you go."
—*Joshua 1:9*, NASB

School opened on Wednesday,
and that was always one of the
happiest days of my life. . . . I
looked around and felt back
home again. Everybody seemed
as glad as I was, scrambling
around, not being able to keep
still, saying hello to one another
and to all the teachers.
—*Ossie Davis*, Just Like Martin

All my life I have worked with youth. I have begged for them and fought for them and lived for them and in them. My story is their story.
—*Mary McLeod Bethune*

Do you see any truly competent workers? They will serve kings rather than ordinary people.
—*Proverbs 22:29, NLT*

Whatever your years, there is in every being's heart the love of wonder, the undaunted challenge of events, the unfailing childlike appetite for what is next, and the joy in the game of life. You are as young as your faith, as old as your fear, as young as your hope, as old as your despair.
—*Douglas MacArthur*

Therefore, my beloved brethren, be steadfast, immovable, always abounding in the work of the Lord, knowing that your toil is not in vain in the Lord.
—*1 Corinthians 15:58, NASB*

Just one act of yours may turn the tide of another person's life.
—*Anonymous*

Our Father, may the world not mold us today, but may we be so strong as to help to mold the world.
—*John Henry Jowett*

Keep your eyes open, hold tight to your convictions, give it all

you've got, be resolute, and love
without stopping.
—*1 Corinthians 16:13, THE MESSAGE*

We teachers can only help the
work going on, as servants wait
upon a master.
—*Maria Montessori*

All service ranks the same with
God.
—*Robert Browning*

Work is the natural exercise and
function of man. . . . Work is not
primarily a thing one does to
live, but the thing one lives to
do. It is, or should be, the full
expression of the worker's fac-
ulties, the thing in which he
finds spiritual, mental, and bod-

ily satisfaction, and the medium in which he offers himself to God.
—*Dorothy L. Sayers*

Problems are only opportunities in work clothes.
—*Henry Kaiser*

Patience and diligence, like faith, remove mountains.
—*William Penn*

My heart is singing for joy this morning. A miracle has happened! The light of understanding has shone upon my little pupil's mind, and behold, all things are changed!
—*Annie Sullivan*

How is it possible that you have not been called? You are already a married man or wife or child or daughter or servant or maid. . . . Nobody is without command and calling. . . . God's eyes look not upon the works, but on the obedience in the work.

—*Martin Luther*

3

LOVING GOD,
LOVING OTHERS

Loving God includes loving people. You've got to love both.
—*1 John 4:21, THE MESSAGE*

He has the right to criticize who
has the heart to help.
—*Abraham Lincoln*

Let your conversation be always
full of grace, seasoned with salt,
so that you may know how to
answer everyone.
—*Colossians 4:6*, NIV

When offering helpful advice,
make it a small helping.
—*Anonymous*

"Don't pick on people, jump on
their failures, criticize their
faults—unless, of course, you
want the same treatment. Don't
condemn those who are down;
that hardness can boomerang.
Be easy on people; you'll find

life a lot easier. Give away your life; you'll find life given back, but not merely given back— given back with bonus and blessing."
—*Luke 6:37-38*, THE MESSAGE

The way I see it, there's always a chance for deep-down good-ness.
—*Sue Diaz, on difficult students, in* Instructor

Children need strength to lean on, a shoulder to cry on, and an example to learn from.
—*Anonymous*

Love each other with brotherly affection and take delight in honoring each other.
—*Romans 12:10,* TLB

"You're blessed when you can show people how to cooperate instead of compete or fight. That's when you discover who you really are, and your place in God's family."
—*Matthew 5:9*, THE MESSAGE

Father, may I so live the life of love this day that all those with whom I have anything to do may be as sure of love in the world as they are of the sunlight.
—*Anonymous*

Do not let any unwholesome talk come out of your mouths, but only what is helpful for building others up according to their needs, that it may benefit those who listen.
—*Ephesians 4:29*, NIV

Religious education, both in the Hebrew and Christian past, had to do with life and living; its motivating force then as now is love . . . [teaching] modeled on love toward God and love toward fellow persons. This brings together both content and action.
—*Robert E. Webber*, Common Roots

Everyone should be quick to listen, slow to speak and slow to become angry, for man's anger does not bring about the righteous life that God desires.
—*James 1:19-20*, NIV

If I speak in the tongues of men and of angels, but have not love, I am a noisy gong or a clanging cymbal. And if I have prophetic powers, and understand all mysteries and all knowledge, and if I have all faith, so as to remove mountains, but have not love, I am nothing. If I give away all I have, and if I deliver my body to be burned, but have not love, I gain nothing. Love is patient and kind; love is not jealous or boastful; it is not arrogant or rude. Love does not insist on its own way; it is not irritable or resentful, it does not rejoice at wrong, but rejoices in the right. Love bears all things, believes all things, hopes all things, endures all things. Love never ends.

—*1 Corinthians 13:1-8, RSV*

Still others have a gift for caring for God's people as a shepherd

does his sheep, leading and teaching them in the ways of God.
—*Ephesians 4:11*, TLB

Disruptive children, slow learners, unattractive children—all were challenges for her to show God's love by being the best teacher she knew how to be.
—*Ruth Beechick*, Teaching Primaries

Patient persistence pierces through indifference; gentle speech breaks down rigid defenses.
—*Proverbs 25:15*, THE MESSAGE

Little children, let us stop just *saying* we love people; let us *really* love them, and show it by our actions. Then we will know for sure, by our actions, that we

are on God's side, and our consciences will be clear, even when we stand before the Lord.
—*1 John 3:18-19*, TLB

A gentle answer turns away wrath, but harsh words stir up anger.
—*Proverbs 15:1*, NLT

Be not angry that you cannot make others as you wish them to be, since you cannot make yourself as you wish to be.
—*Thomas à Kempis*

Be kind and compassionate to one another, forgiving each other, just as in Christ God forgave you.
—*Ephesians 4:32*, NIV

Do not withhold good from those who deserve it, when it is in your power to act.
—*Proverbs 3:27, NIV*

When kids feel right, they'll behave right. How do we help them feel right? By accepting their feelings!
—*Adele Faber and Elaine Mazlish,* How to Talk So Kids Can Learn

Each one should use whatever gift he has received to serve others, faithfully administering God's grace in its various forms. If anyone speaks, he should do it as one speaking the very words of God. If anyone serves, he should do it with the strength God provides, so that in all things God may be praised

through Jesus Christ. To him be
the glory and the power forever
and ever. Amen.
—*1 Peter 4:10-11, NIV*

Teach with a servant attitude
rather than an authoritarian
one.
- -*Joan M. Dungey*

You should be like one happy
family, full of sympathy toward
each other, loving one another
with tender hearts and humble
minds.
—*1 Peter 3:8, TLB*

And let us consider how we may
spur one another on toward love
and good deeds.
—*Hebrews 10:24, NIV*

A cheerful heart is good medicine, but a broken spirit saps a person's strength.
—*Proverbs 17:22, NLT*

When we set a standard and model courteous behavior, students learn that good manners are not ends in themselves, but are aspects of caring and respect.
—*William J. Kreidler*

Let the word of Christ dwell in you richly as you teach and admonish one another with all wisdom, and as you sing psalms, hymns and spiritual songs with gratitude in your hearts to God. And whatever you do, whether in word or deed, do it all in the name of the

Lord Jesus, giving thanks to God the Father through him.
—*Colossians 3:16-17*, NIV

You can give without loving, but you cannot love without giving.
—*Amy Carmichael*

There is no exercise better for the heart than reaching down and lifting people up.
—*John Andrew Holmer*

The mark of a man is how he treats a person who can be of no possible use to him.
—*Anonymous*

If you want to change people without giving offense or arousing resentment, use encourage-

ment. Make the fault you want to correct seem easy to correct; make the thing you want the other person to do seem easy to do. . . . If you and I will inspire the people with whom we come in contact to a realization of the hidden treasures they possess, we can do far more than change people. We can literally transform them.
—*Dale Carnegie*

There ain't much fun in medicine, but there's a good deal of medicine in fun.
—*Josh Billings*

Good words quench more than a bucket of water.
—*George Herbert*

4

GOD'S GIFT OF WISDOM

Finally, brothers, whatever is true, whatever is noble, whatever is right, whatever is pure, whatever is lovely, whatever is admirable . . . think about such things.
—*Philippians 4:8, NIV*

He established a decree in Jacob,
and appointed a law in Israel,
which he commanded our
    ancestors
to teach to their children;
that the next generation might
    know them,
the children yet unborn,
and rise up and tell them to
    their children,
so that they should set their
    hope in God.
—*Psalm 78:5-7, NRSV*

Your word is a lamp for my feet
and a light for my path.
—*Psalm 119:105, NLT*

Happy and blessed is that person whom truth teacheth and informeth.
—*Thomas à Kempis*

Give discernment to me, your
servant; then I will understand
your decrees. As your words are
taught, they give light! Even the
simple can understand them.
—*Psalm 119:125, 130,* NLT

Light another person's candle
by your own and you will not
lose any of the brilliancy by
what the other gains.
—*Jo Petty,* Words of Silver and Gold

Form your purpose by asking
for counsel, then carry it out using all the help you can get.
—*Proverbs 20:18,* THE MESSAGE

Our vision for education has always been to actively engage
students in content, application,

and calling. . . . We expect our students to use their knowledge to serve God and their neighbor.
—*Robert Thayer, school administrator, quoted in* Christian Home & School

I will instruct you (says the Lord) and guide you along the best pathway for your life; I will advise you and watch your progress.
—*Psalm 32:8,* TLB

Lord, speak to me; and then speak through me.
—*Anonymous*

And what do we teach our children in school? We teach them that two and two make four, and that Paris is the capital of France.

When will we also teach them what they are?

You should say to each of them: "Do you know what you are? You are a marvel. You are unique. In all the world there is no other child exactly like you. In the millions of years that have passed there has never been a child like you. And look at your body—what a wonder it is! Your legs, your arms, your cunning fingers, the way you move! You may become a Shakespeare, a Michelangelo, a Beethoven. You have the capacity for anything. Yes, you are a marvel."
—*Pablo Casals*

Anyone who gets so progressive in his thinking that he walks out

on the teaching of Christ, walks out on God.
—*2 John 9*, THE MESSAGE

Intelligent people are always open to new ideas. In fact, they look for them.
—*Proverbs 18:15*, NLT

Rules that control, rather than inform, can kill creativity.
—*Teresa M. Amabile*, Growing Up Creative

Have nothing to do with godless myths and old wives' tales; rather, train yourself to be godly. For physical training is of some value, but godliness has value for all things, holding promise

for both the present life and the
life to come.
—*1 Timothy 4:7-8, NIV*

Teach your children to choose the
right path, and when they are
older, they will remain upon it.
—*Proverbs 22:6, NLT*

O God . . . Save us from slipshod
or dishonest thinking. Forbid
that we should turn away from
any question, either because we
do not know, or because we fear
to give, the answer. . . . Strengthen
us to read and think and work
with courage and humility, con-
fident that if we seek the truth
we shall not lack the guidance of
thy Spirit; through Jesus Christ
our Lord.
—*A New Prayer Book*

Behold, Thou dost desire truth in the innermost being, and in the hidden part Thou wilt make me know wisdom.
—*Psalm 51:6, NASB*

Imagination is more important than knowledge.
—*Albert Einstein*

Whoever walks with the wise will become wise; whoever walks with fools will suffer harm.
—*Proverbs 13:20, NLT*

It's not so much what is poured into the student, but what is planted, that really counts.
—Anonymous

He who trusts in himself is a fool, but he who walks in wisdom is kept safe.
—*Proverbs 28:26, NIV*

How can a young person stay pure? By obeying your word and following its rules.
—*Psalm 119:9, NLT*

Your principles have been the music of my life throughout the years of my pilgrimage. I reflect at night on who you are, O Lord, and I obey your law because of this. This is my happy way of life: obeying your commandments.
—*Psalm 119:54-56, NLT*

By wisdom a house is built, and by understanding it is estab-

lished; by knowledge the rooms
are filled with all precious and
pleasant riches.
—*Proverbs 24:3-4, RSV*

It has always seemed strange to
me that in our endless discus-
sions about education so little
stress is ever laid on the pleasure
of becoming an educated person, the enormous interest it
adds to life.
—*Edith Hamilton*

To discipline a child is not to
punish him for stepping out of
line, but to teach that child the
way he ought to go. Discipline
therefore includes everything
that you do in order to help children learn.
—*Henry R. Brandt*

It's a great mistake, I think, to put children off with falsehoods and nonsense, when their growing powers of observation and discrimination excite in them a desire to know about things.
—*Annie Sullivan*

The point of having an open mind, like having an open mouth, is to close it on something solid.
—*G. K. Chesterton*

A free curiosity is more effective in learning than a rigid discipline.
—*Augustine of Hippo*

An education isn't how much you have committed to memory,

or even how much you know. It's being able to differentiate between what you do know and what you don't. It's knowing where to go to find out what you need to know; and it's knowing how to use the information once you get it.

—*William Feather*

5

TO REST IN THE LORD

At day's end I'm ready for sound sleep, for you have put my life back together.
—*Psalm 4:8, THE MESSAGE*

"Come to me, all who labor and
are heavy laden, and I will give
you rest."
—*Matthew 11:28, RSV*

He gives power to the weak,
And to those who have no
　　might
　He increases strength.
Even the youth shall faint
　and be weary,
And the young men shall
　　utterly fall,
But those who wait on the Lord
Shall renew their strength;
They shall mount up with
　　wings like eagles,
They shall run and not be
　　weary,
They shall walk and not faint.
—*Isaiah 40:29-31, NKJV*

Father, today I felt your presence in the classroom. By faith I know that you are always there. But thank you for those times which *confirm* that in you we live and move and have our being.
—*Elsbeth Campbell Murphy,*
Chalkdust: Prayer Meditations for Teachers

Rejoice in the Lord always. I will say it again: Rejoice! Let your gentleness be evident to all. The Lord is near. Do not be anxious about anything, but in everything, by prayer and petition, with thanksgiving, present your requests to God. And the peace of God, which transcends all understanding, will guard your hearts and your minds in Christ Jesus.
—*Philippians 4:4-7, NIV*

The Lord is my light and my salvation—so why should I be afraid? The Lord protects me from danger—so why should I tremble?

—*Psalm 27:1, NLT*

The peace of Christ is the peace of trust in the cause we serve, even when our service seems inadequate. It is the peace of confidence in God when everything seems to be working toward ungodly ends; it is the peace of those who struggle to see immediate success from their efforts and yet can still believe that God overrules their failures for good.

—*William Adams Brown, adapted*

I can do all things through Christ who strengthens me.
—*Philippians 4:13, NKJV*

Have courage for the great sorrows of life and patience for the small ones; and when you have laboriously accomplished your daily task, go to sleep in peace. God is awake.
—*Victor Hugo*

For I am sure that neither death, nor life, nor angels, nor principalities, nor things present, nor things to come, nor powers, nor height, nor depth, nor anything else in all creation will be able to separate us from the love of God in Christ Jesus our Lord.
—*Romans 8:38-39, RSV*

Take courage ... for I am with you,
says the Lord of hosts ... my Spirit
abides among you; fear not.
—*Haggai 2:4, RSV*

He will never let me stumble,
slip or fall. For he is always
watching, never sleeping. Jeho-
vah himself is caring for you! He
is your defender. He protects
you day and night. He keeps
you from all evil, and preserves
your life. He keeps his eye upon
you as you come and go, and
always guards you.
—*Psalm 121:3-8, TLB*

You are my hiding place; you
will protect me from trouble
and surround me with songs of
deliverance.
—*Psalm 32:7, NIV*

Peace *with* God brings the peace *of* God. It is a peace that settles our nerves, fills our mind, floods our spirit, and in the midst of the uproar around us, gives us the assurance that everything is all right.
—*Bob Mumford*

Every morning I open the window for my King's grace, and every evening I sleep upon the pillow of his love and care.
—*Celtic saint*